990820824 1

WITHDRAWN

First published in the U.K. in 1993 by
Evans Brothers Limited,
2A Portman Mansions,
Chiltern Street,
London W1M 1LE

First published in Australia in 1992 by
Macmillan Education Australia Pty. Ltd.,
107 Moray Street, South Melbourne 3205
6 Clarke Street, Crows Nest 2065

Copyright © Harry Breidahl 1992
Illustrations by Sharyn Madder

All rights reserved. No part of this publication may be reproduced, stored in a retrieval system, or transmitted, in any form or by any means, electronic, mechanical, photocopying, recording, or otherwise, without prior permission of Evans Brothers Limited.

ISBN 0 237 51303 X

Set in Helvetica and Times Roman by
CAPS & lowercase, Australia
Printed in Hong Kong

What's the Difference?

Butterflies and Moths

Written by Harry Breidahl * Illustrated by Sharyn Madder

Contents

Butterflies and Moths	2
What's the Difference?	4
By Day and By Night	6
Insects	8
Invertebrates	10
Being a Butterfly or Moth	12
Butterfly and Moth Lifetimes	14
Caterpillars	16
Pupa, Chrysalis and Cocoon	18
Butterfly and Moth History	20
Butterfly and Moth Conservation	22
Glossary	24
Index	

Butterflies and Moths

Butterflies and moths are among the most beautiful and easily recognised of insects. They come in an almost endless variety of colours, shapes and sizes.

Orchard Swallowtail Butterfly

Common Grass Blue Butterfly

Indian Leaf Butterfly

Postman Butterfly

Metallic Moth

Emperor Gum Moth

Eltham Copper Butterfly

Oleander Hawk Moth

Pericopine Moth

3

What's the Difference?

There are many things that can be used to tell the difference between a butterfly and a moth.

Moth

Butterfly

4

Butterflies	Moths
Usually hold their wings over their backs when resting. 	Usually hold their wings flat when resting. 
Have knobs on the end of their antennae. 	Have feather-like or plain antennae. 
Don't have their front and back wings joined together. 	Have their front and back wings joined by rows of small spines and hooks. 

By Day and By Night

Butterflies are generally brightly coloured and active during the day, while most moths are dull coloured and fly by night.

Although they rest with their wings folded up, butterflies often spread their wings out to warm-up in the sun.

Orange Jezabel Butterfly

Many butterflies have a different colour pattern on the top and on the underneath of their wings.

Moths are often seen fluttering around an outside light or bumping into windows at night.

Because they fly at night, moths cannot warm themselves in the sun. Some moths are covered in hairy scales that keep them warm.

Most night-flying moths are dull coloured so that they can hide during the day.

Privet Hawk Moth

Insects

Butterflies and moths belong to a group of animals called insects.

Most insects have wings.

All insects bodies are divided into three parts: a head, a thorax and an abdomen.

Insects breathe through small holes in their sides.

Insects have two antennae which are used for smelling and feeling.

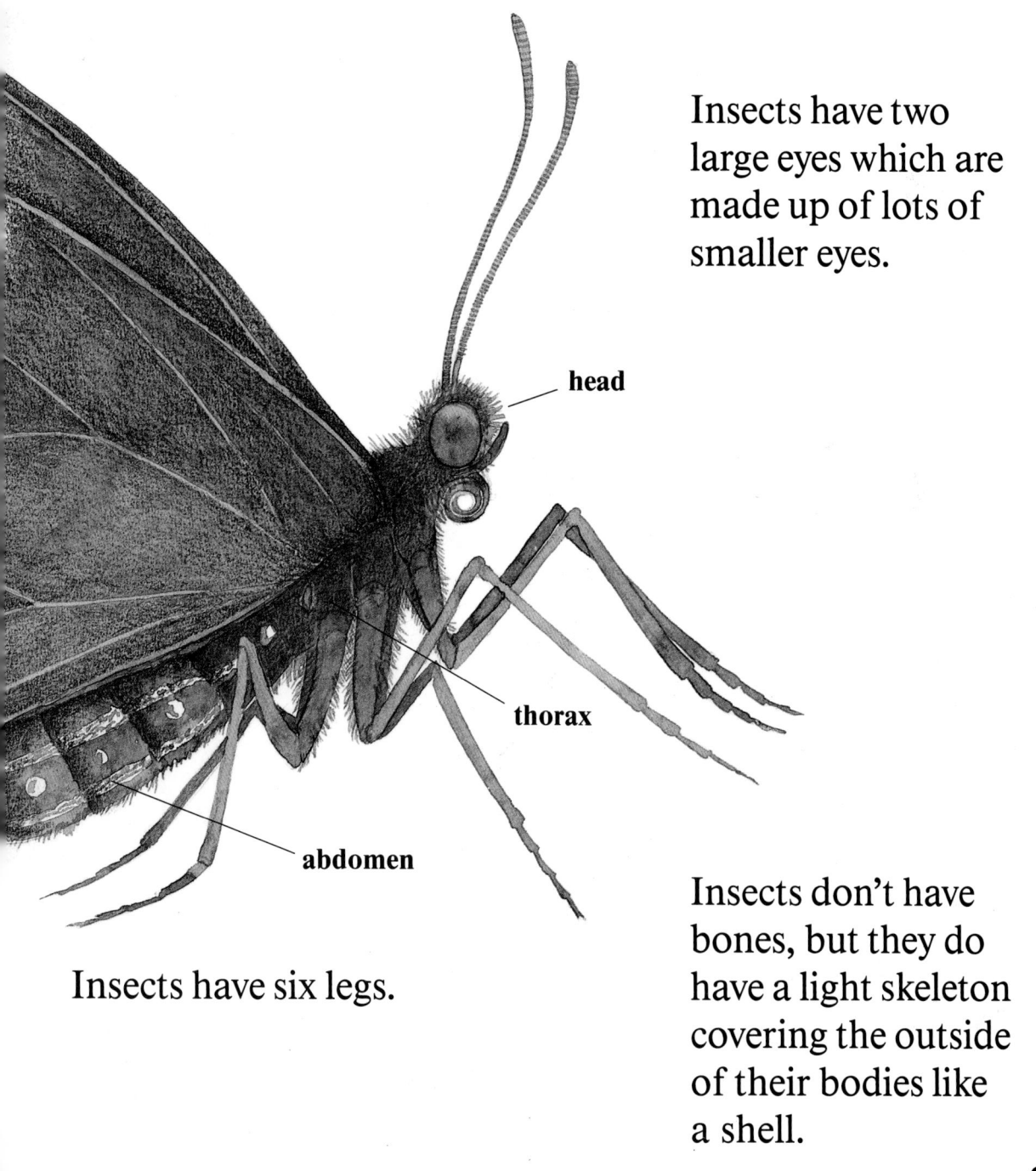

Insects have two large eyes which are made up of lots of smaller eyes.

head

thorax

abdomen

Insects have six legs.

Insects don't have bones, but they do have a light skeleton covering the outside of their bodies like a shell.

9

Invertebrates

Invertebrates are animals without backbones. Insects are invertebrates. There are many other kinds of invertebrates. All of these animals are invertebrates, but they are not all insects.

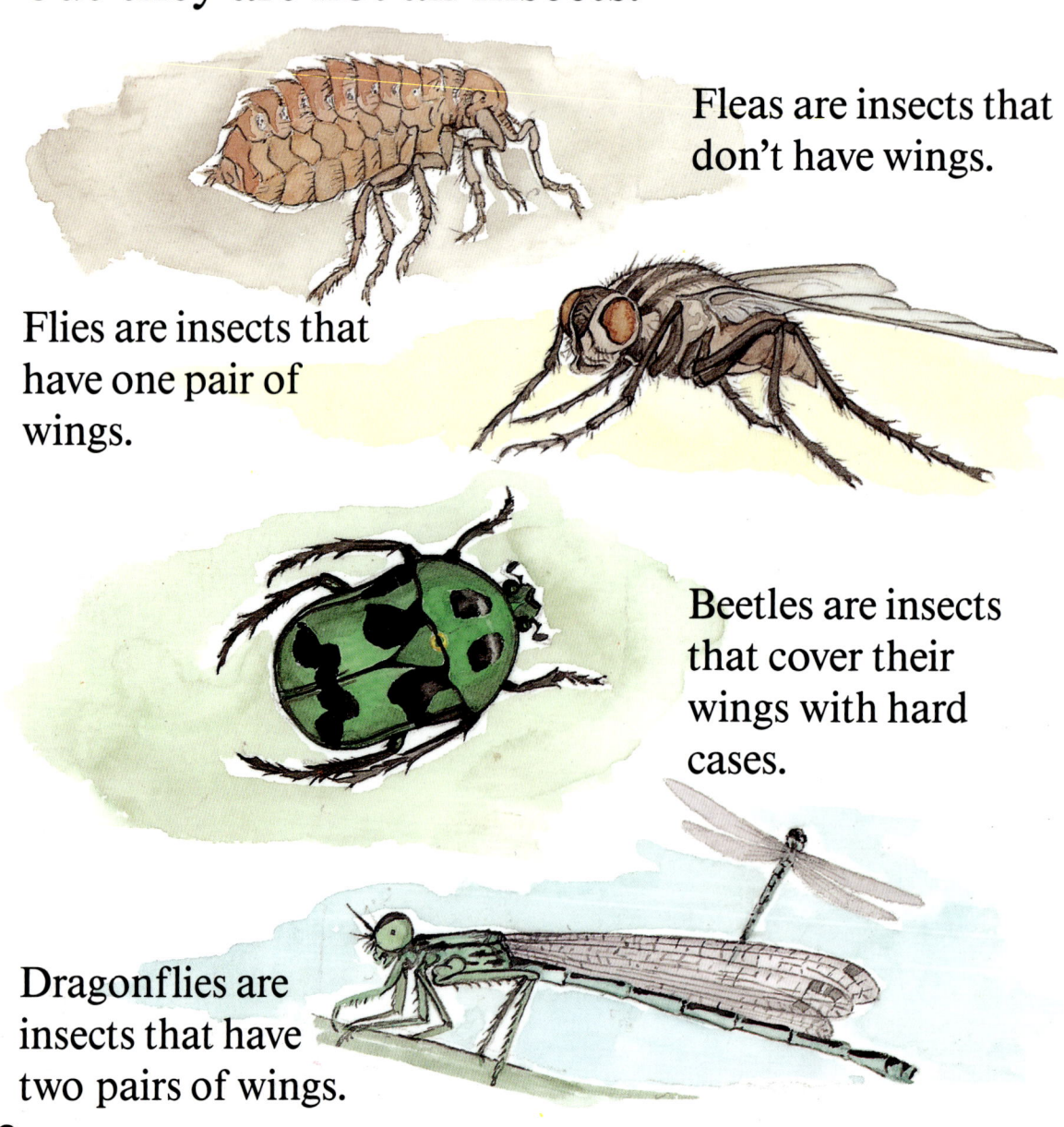

Fleas are insects that don't have wings.

Flies are insects that have one pair of wings.

Beetles are insects that cover their wings with hard cases.

Dragonflies are insects that have two pairs of wings.

Spiders are not insects because they have eight legs.

Millipedes are not insects because they have many legs.

Crabs are not insects because they have eight legs and two nippers.

Earthworms are not insects because they have no legs and no skeleton.

Being a Butterfly or Moth

A number of things make butterflies and moths different from all other insects.

A butterfly or moth has four large wings: a pair of front wings and a pair of back wings.

Butterflies' and moths' wings and bodies are covered in small scales. These scales come off easily, so only handle butterflies and moths with great care.

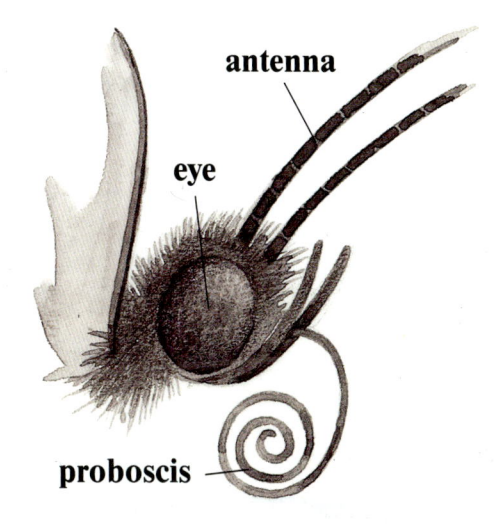

front wings

back wings

antenna

eye

proboscis

All butterflies and most moths feed by drinking through a straw-like tube called a proboscis (say *pro-boss-kiss*). The proboscis is coiled when not in use.

Butterfly and Moth Lifetimes

Insects have a number of stages in their life. The first stage of a butterfly's or moth's life is an egg. The caterpillar that hatches from this egg must do a lot of eating before it can change into an adult butterfly or moth.

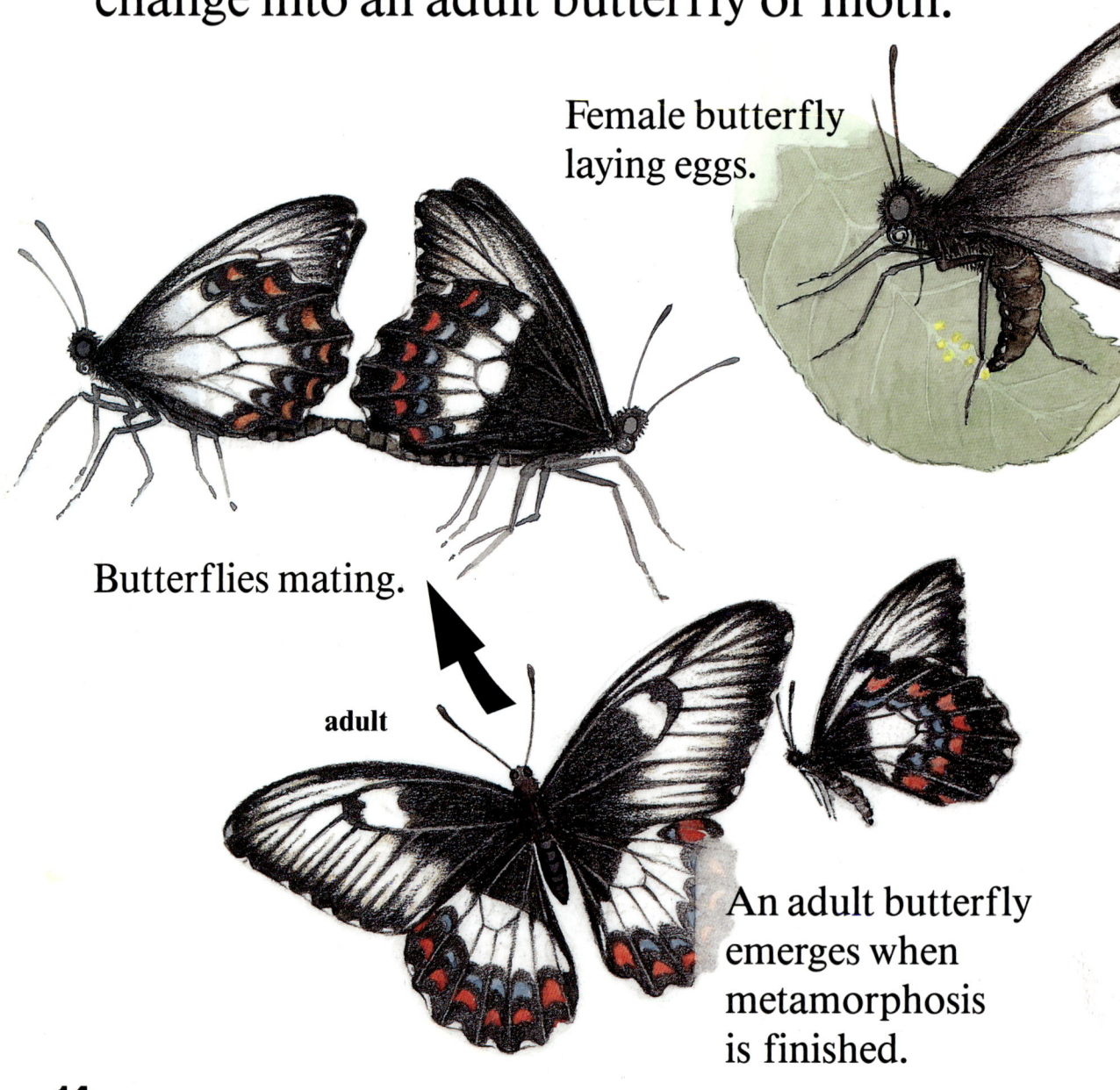

Female butterfly laying eggs.

Butterflies mating.

adult

An adult butterfly emerges when metamorphosis is finished.

Life cycle of a butterfly

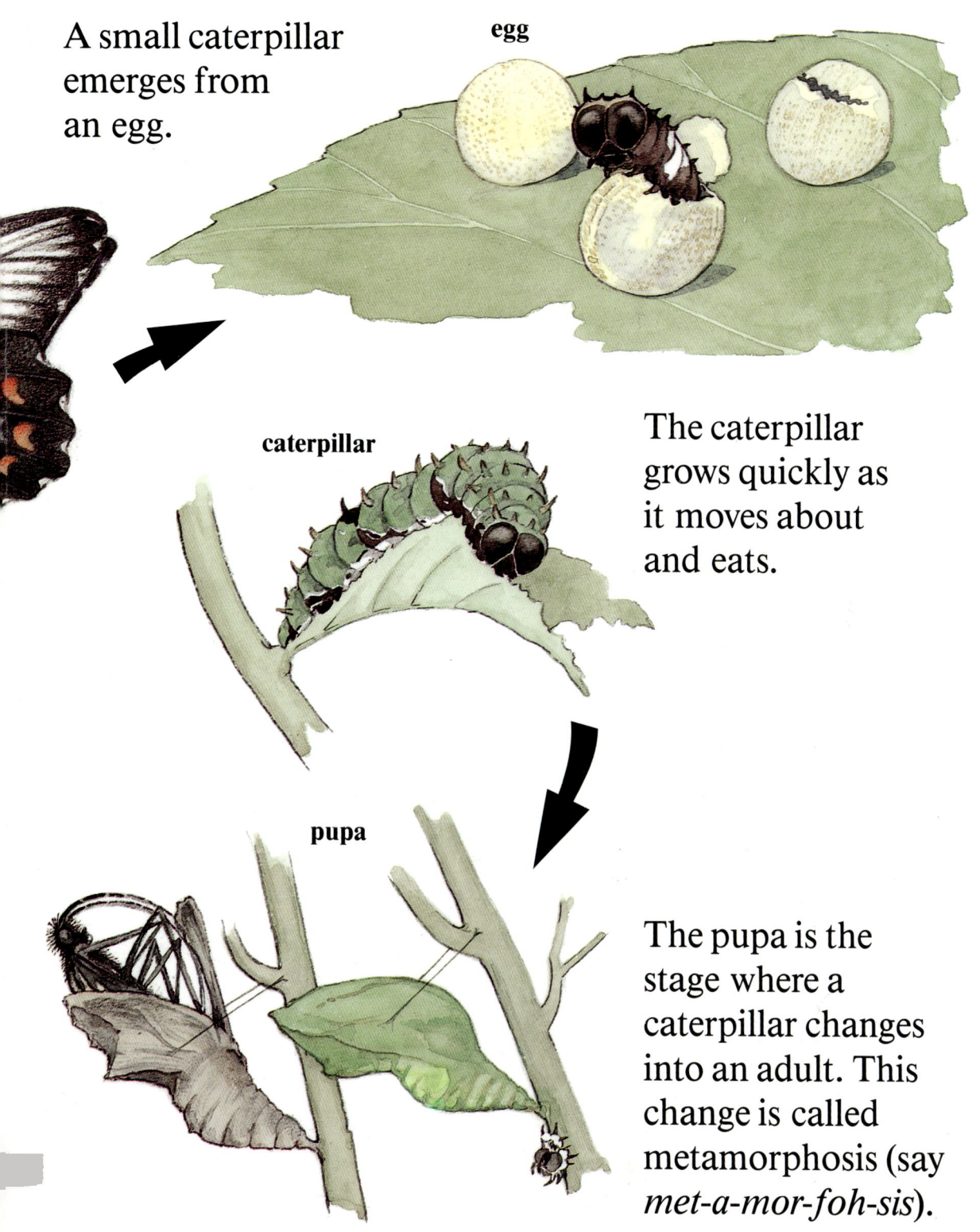

A small caterpillar emerges from an egg.

egg

caterpillar

The caterpillar grows quickly as it moves about and eats.

pupa

The pupa is the stage where a caterpillar changes into an adult. This change is called metamorphosis (say *met-a-mor-foh-sis*).

Caterpillars

Caterpillars spend most of their time feeding on leaves and grass. All of this eating leads to a caterpillar that is big enough to change into a pupa and then into an adult butterfly or moth.

Many caterpillars are brightly coloured to warn predators that they are poisonous.

abdomen

Like the butterfly or moth into which it will change, a caterpillar's body is divided into head, thorax and abdomen.

Seen from underneath, a caterpillar has six "true" legs on its thorax and up to ten "prolegs" on its abdomen.

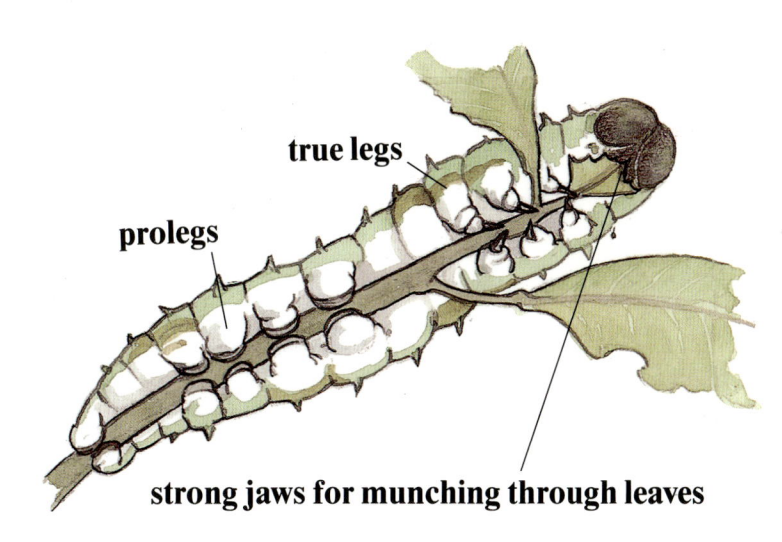

true legs
prolegs
strong jaws for munching through leaves

thorax

head

Butterfly caterpillars always have ten prolegs, moth caterpillars may have less than ten.

Pupa, Chrysalis and Cocoon

As a caterpillar grows it peels off old layers of skin. When it is time for metamorphosis, the caterpillar peels off one last layer of skin to uncover the next stage in its life, called the pupa.

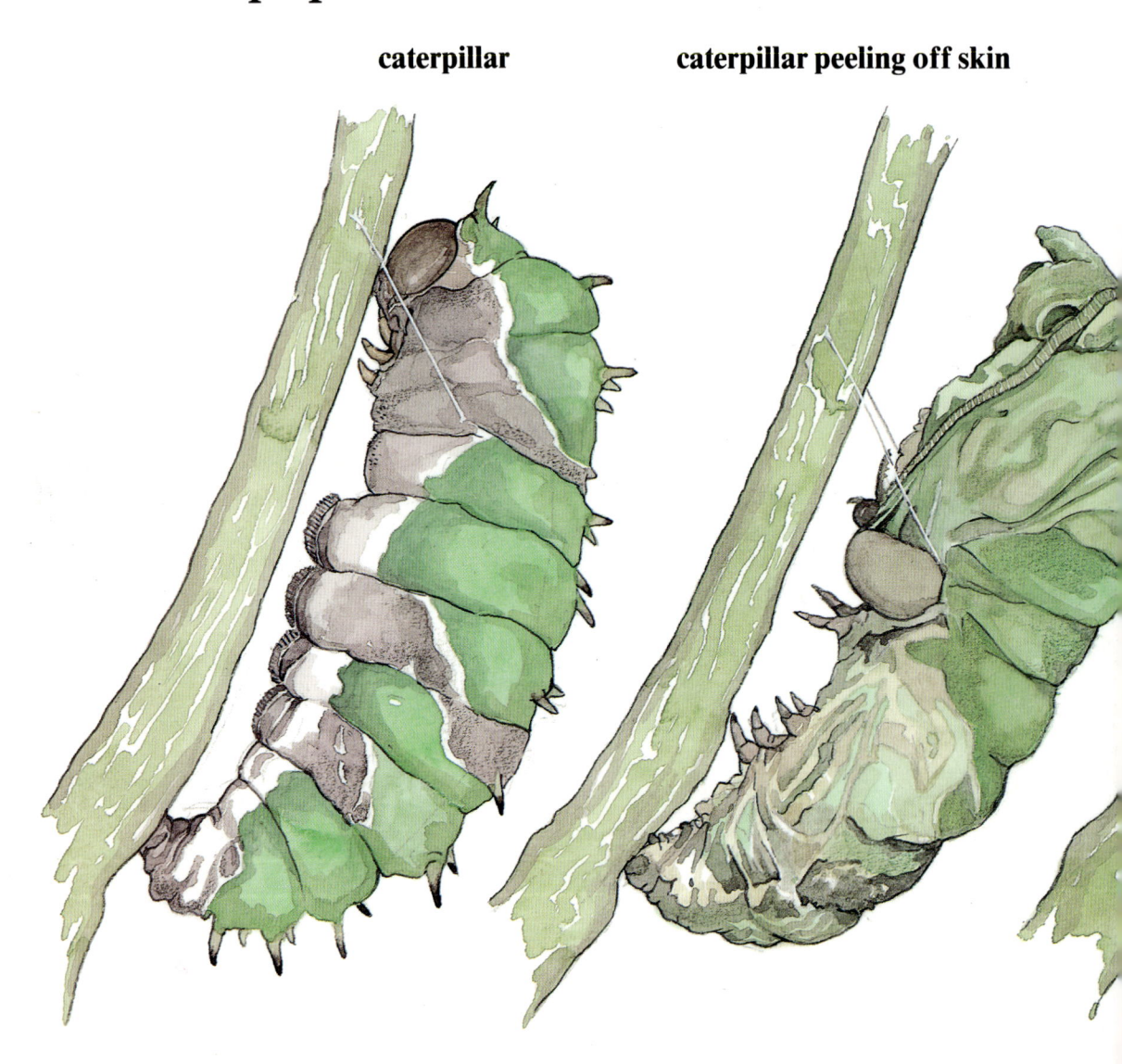

caterpillar

caterpillar peeling off skin

Moth caterpillars usually make a silk cocoon before they form a chrysalis but butterfly caterpillars don't.

the pupa inside a case called a chrysalis

butterfly emerging

19

Butterfly and Moth History

Although there has been life in the sea for billions of years, plants and animals first appeared on land about 420 million years ago. Insects were among the first animals to make this move onto the land.

The early swamps of the Age of Amphibians were home to giant dragonflies and cockroaches as well as giant amphibians.

Moths first appeared on earth about 140 million years ago. These moths shared the world with dinosaurs during the Age of Reptiles.

Butterfly and Moth Conservation

People who study insects are called entomologists (say *en-toe-mol-o-jists*). Many entomologists are worried about the number of butterflies and moths that are in danger of becoming extinct.

This Californian Xerces Blue Butterfly is extinct. This means that it has vanished forever.

The Queen Alexandra's Birdwing Butterfly is endangered by the clearing of its forests and by butterfly collectors.

This Philippines Swallowtail Butterfly was discovered in the last few years, but is already endangered.

The rare Eltham Copper Butterfly was endangered when people wanted to build houses in the only area where it is found. The houses were not built and the Eltham Copper's habitat is now protected.

Glossary

Antennae A whip-like structure on the head of some invertebrates. It is used for the senses of touch and smell.

Caterpillar The worm-like grub that hatches out of an insect egg.

Chrysalis The case in which a caterpillar changes into a butterfly or moth.

Cocoon A protective covering for an insect pupa.

Endangered A word used to describe a plant or animal that will soon become extinct if it is not protected.

Extinct A word used to describe an animal or plant that is no longer living.

Habitat Any place where an animal or plant naturally lives.

Insect An invertebrate animal with a light skeleton on the outside, six legs, and a body divided into three parts: head, thorax and abdomen.

Metamorphosis The process where a caterpillar changes into a butterfly or moth.

Predator An animal that catches and eats another animal.

Proboscis A long straw-like tube with which butterflies and moths 'drink' their food.

Prolegs Leg-like structures on the abdomen of a caterpillar. They are not present in the adult stage.

Pupa The stage in an insect's life when it changes from a caterpillar into an adult.

True legs Legs on the thorax of an insect. They are present in both the caterpillar and adult stages.

Index

Age of Amphibians 20
Age of Reptiles 21
antennae 5, 9

backbone 10
beetle 10

Californian Xerces Blue Butterfly 22
caterpillar 14, 15, 16-17, 18, 19
chrysalis 19
cockroach 20
cocoon 19
conservation 22
crab 11

dinosaur 21
dragonfly 10, 20

earthworm 11
eggs 14, 15
Eltham Copper Butterfly 23
entomologist 22

flea 10
fly 10

insects 2, 8-9, 10, 11, 12, 14, 20
invertebrate 10

metamorphosis 14, 15, 18
millipede 11

Philippines Swallowtail Butterfly 23
proboscis 13
prolegs 17
pupa 15, 16, 18

Queen Alexandra's Birdwing
    Butterfly 22

scales 7, 13
skeleton 9
spider 11

true legs 17

wings 5, 6, 8, 12